T0345795

Saint Petersburg Notebook

Saint Petersburg Notebook

Ann Lauterbach

OMNIDAWN PUBLISHING
RICHMOND, CALIFORNA
2014

Cover and interior photos by Ann Lauterbach.

Cover and interior design by Peter Burghardt.

Typefaces: Avenir LT Standard, Century Schoolbook.

Printed in the United States
On Roland 55# Natural Enviro Book 100% PCW
Acid Free Archival Quality Paper
with Rainbow FSC Certified Colored End Papers

Published by Omnidawn Publishing, Richmond, California
www.omnidawn.com   (510) 237-5472   (800) 792-4957
10 9 8 7 6 5 4 3 2 1
ISBN: 978-1-890650-76-6

In memory of my father
Richard E. Lauterbach
(1914-1950)

But the holy city of Peter
Will be an unwitting monument to us.

Anna Akhmatova, "Petrograd 1919"

INTRODUCTION : The Untranslatable

1. MEANWHILE

I've been listening to Pandora radio, set to the Bob
Dylan station, now playing Jimi Hendrix singing "Like
a Rolling Stone." The sound seems distorted on all the
songs, as if filtered so many times it has lost some sonic
ingredient, whatever it is that makes music specific
to memory's aural imprint. I have huge old Yamaha
speakers, so perhaps it's that the digital radio doesn't
want to be exposed to speakers that were created for
analog sound.

Before I was listening to Pandora, I was reading Herta
Müller's 2009 novel *The Hunger Angel*, sent to me by a
young German friend, along with Müller's Nobel Prize
acceptance speech. Both of these writings are acutely
spare, like sharp needles that pierce to the core and
leave tiny soul scars. In the case of the novel, the *core*
is depredations of exile; specifically, exile from Roma-
nia in 1945 to work in the Russian labor camps. The
book is narrated by its protagonist Leo Auberg and Leo
is based on the life of Oskar Pastior, the Romanian-
born German-speaking poet (and member of Oulipo;
translated by Harry Mathews, published by Burning
Deck). Herta Müller had spent many hours in con-
versation with Pastior; they had intended to publish
a collaboration, but he died in 2006, before this could
happen. Instead, she wrote *The Hunger Angel*.

Müller's novel has made me think about the relation between actual experience and memory, and memory and the imagination; about the relation between duration and endurance within physical and mental realms of life; about the complex arena of translation in its broadest sense. I have thought of these things often over many years, so I am returning to them.

There is a passage in *The Hunger Angel* about shoveling coal with a heart-shaped shovel. It's an account of physical movement, set against or into a near absolute void caused by the body's hunger and the spirit's depletion. In her Nobel speech, Müller speaks about the sound of language in relation to material objects and to emotional gesture. She writes,

"The sound of the words knows that it has no choice but to beguile, because objects deceive with their materials, and feelings mislead with their gestures. The sound of the words, along with the truth this sound invents, resides at the interface, where the deceit of the materials and that of the gestures come together. In writing, it is not a matter of trusting, but rather the honesty of the deceit."

These delicate coordinates captured, as Müller says, by the poetics of sound, animate our awareness of what it means to elucidate the historical real as imagined presence.

2. SLS

In 2006, I was invited to join the Summer Literary Seminars session in Saint Petersburg, Russia.

The Summer Literary Seminars (SLS) was founded in 1998 by the Russian-born writer Mikhail Iossel, who immigrated to the United States in 1986, and subsequently moved to Canada. Misha, as he is sometimes called, started SLS in part because it would enable him, as he puts it, "to go back to the place of my origins, in my new capacity of an Anglophone writer, without having to pay the air fare." Then, as now, SLS ran on a proverbial shoe-string, but it has grown and expanded, attracting to its faculty writers from the US, Canada, Russia, Europe and East Africa. It meets now in Lithuania, as well as in Kenya and Montreal. A small group of English-speaking students travels to the designated place to study with selected writing faculty, while simultaneously exploring the host city. There are lectures and tours and readings and classes, all jammed into a few intense weeks. One segment of these activities is devoted to "the untranslatable," talks on those obdurate but inexhaustible conditions of intimate knowledge—of a self, a history, a place—from which so much creative work arises.

There were a number of younger poets who were part the SLS group that summer, including Anna Moschovakis, Matvei Yankelevich, and Genya Turovskaya. I already knew Anna and Genya, both of whom had been students in the Bard Master of Arts Program, where I have taught since the early 1990s. Matvei and Anna are founding members of the publishing collective Ugly Duckling Presse; they are accomplished poets as well as translators (and both now also teach with me in the Bard MFA). Eugene Ostashevsky (also called Genya) was with us, a tall, shambly, wry and widely knowledgeable poet whose presence was always reassuring, as well as Matthew Zapruder, one of the founders of Wave Books. These energetic and informed persons kept me from feeling entirely estranged, from myself as well as from my surroundings.

3. THE RUSSIAN CONNECTION—

I had never been to Russia. My parents had eloped there in the 1930s, both while on undergraduate trips, and my father had become a foreign correspondent for *Time* magazine from Moscow during World War II. He wrote three journalistic books about Russia before he died in 1950.

When I was in college, I began to study Russian, thinking I would become a translator, but I gave up, which I regret to this day, leaving me with a few truncated phrases. When I lived in London in the 1970s, there was an active interest in non-Anglo poetry and poetics. (While I was working at the Institute of Contemporary Arts, I arranged a series of readings and lectures on recent French, East European and American poetry, called "Poetry Information.") In London, I discovered the poetry of Anna Akhmatova and Marina Tsvetaeva (the latter was translated by the English poet Elaine Feinstein, the same poet who wrote to Charles Olson asking about Projective Verse). Daniel Weissbort and Ted Hughes edited the magazine *Modern Poetry in Translation*, whose Number 6, from 1970, was dedicated to Russian poets and writers, including Sergei Esenin, Daniil Kharms, Alexander Blok and Tsvetaeva.

Back home in New York, I read Joseph Brodsky's luminous essays collected in *Less than One* (1986) and Nadezhda Mandelstam's memoir *Hope Against Hope* (1970). I began to better comprehend the personal, political and cultural ravages that many of these poets had undergone. They became ghostly, attenuated companions, echoes without originals, but with searing linguistic presences for me, even in translation. They came to exemplify the urgencies of the Modernist poetic avant-garde; I understood that some formal innovations are acts of resistance and subversive necessity. The early 20th-century Russian painters, especially Malevich and Kandinsky, had been crucial to my discovery that abstraction could be seen as a search for a universal visual language, hovering near (or indebted to) but averting the possibility of transcendence.

4. RECKONING

While on the SLS trip I realized how difficult it is for
me to be part of a group; that is, the fact of this dif-
ficulty became more exposed, more bluntly apparent.
This tendency goes very far back into my early life,
when I began to find the pleasures of solitude as a
way to escape the turbulent vagaries of an unreliable
and often threatening household. I had not so much a
desire to run away as a desire to be lost, *elsewhere*, to
find myself exempt from the logistical norms of time
and place. When I began to paint, and later, when I
began to write, I realized that *making* something could
change clock time into an immeasurable temporal field
of absorbed attention.

I didn't want to join either cliques or teams; I hated
competitive sports, and I feared gangs. It is possible
that anxious grown-up talk in the house around Left
politics may have seeped into my mind; the atmo-
sphere seemed to thicken ominously both while my
father lived and after he died, when McCarthyism was
in full brutal tilt. Perhaps the idea of *joining* seemed
innately dangerous; there was talk of betrayal, there
was something unnamed and immense shadowing the
bright idealisms taught at my small progressive school,
with its internationalist zeal and belief in the arts.
Language is contagious, especially when one is young
and alert, listening and watching for imminent harm.
Somehow the notion of autonomy emerged as the least
compromised mode of personal evolution; even now, I

seem unable to distinguish between productive habit and blind coercion. It's a daily quandary.

I like the focus of singular conversations, that is, conversations with a single person. Perhaps this is simply a projection of an ideal reader, a utopian vision of concentrated reciprocity. In any case, this temperamental disinclination to join has made me generally speaking a poor citizen if at times a good observer. I would have made an excellent *flaneur*. I love the specific urban experience of anonymity, of watching fellow humans move through and across space, marking the exquisite difference between internal thought and external motions and behaviors which language seeks to measure and articulate, threading our subjectivities to the world. I love the sense that I am part of this flow, these passages of mortal syntax.

I kept the Notebook intermittently, as an attempt to close the gap between seeing and saying, being alone and being among.

December 2013

Saint Petersburg Notebook
Does The Bear Eat Masha? I Cannot Remember

SUNDAY (11 JUNE 2006)

Loud chirps.

Building a large pale, dirty yellow, looming around a courtyard; cement façade. Stairs wide uneven stone.

Long corridors with thin red carpet.

Furniture minimal, crummy, as if everything had come from a former dorm or from a flea market or from Ikea after Ikea; old Ikea.

Sound porous, the materials porous.

Decor gestures are meager; a curtain here, a light fixture there, but a profound sense of an erased cultural memory; whatever might be thought of as comfortable or nice is not to be found here as material presence.

Yet not as if it were all about the life of the mind; it isn't about choices made but clearly about necessity. One feels the strain and violence of change even now, with late stage capitalism moving in on late stage State repression and causing a sort of grim collision.

The persons on the street are quick moving, but one intuits a distrust or fear or lack of interest in strangers. This must be part of the cultural hangover.

No pictures on the walls.

MONDAY

Yesterday walked to the theatere to get tickets for the ballet and back along the Nevsky Prospect. Bright sun.

Petersburg was built in the early eighteenth century by Peter the Great to emulate European cities (Rome and Amsterdam, oddly), with wide avenues or boulevards, buildings set back, bridges over canals and across the river. It is not as intimate as Paris nor as grand as London nor as quaint as Amsterdam, but has some resemblances to each of them. The long daylight is remarkable and disorienting; difficult to believe that it is ten at night, when it appears to be two or three in the afternoon, as if the earth had slowed down, the sun stilled: trance light. I did not go on the boat trip last night, even though it was a perfect night for it, but let myself down into sleep in the tiny narrow nun's bed.

The Senior dinner at Bard's Smolny College was great fun, at least in terms of watching people; the young women dressed to kill—really, with wild, flamboyantly sexual outfits but with so little attitude or sophistication attached that it all seemed like a costume ball.

Many of them are beautiful, and there seems little sense of one notion of how to look, which is a relief after the fashionistas of New York. There was one young woman in a backless, tight, crimson dress, which she occasionally pulled at, hitching it down, in a gesture of beguiling unselfconsciousness. Very few men, and they seemingly nearly invisible to the women; at one point there was dancing, and the young women let out a great cry and formed a circle and danced that famous folk dance I remember learning in grade school, although I have forgotten the name of it.

Two long banquet tables were laid out. White cloths, glasses arranged, and many plates of finger food, most of which involve small pastry cups filled with something: tiny cups of caviar, a delicious mushroom/cheese hot mixture, chicken salad, and so forth; red, rosé, white wines, and small glasses of vodka. Another table with desserts, massive and creamy.

I had a long talk with a young man earlier about Russia, trying to get some purchase on what is happening, has happened. I am really ignorant, although feel strong currents of fragmented knowledge; scraps. The country is, like America, culturally belated, maybe because of conflicting cultural strands as well as its vast land mass. Modernity—is that what I mean?—or is it Modernism itself?—one feels that Russia created the conditions, but that it has come late and piecemeal, without a clear historical necessity. In any event, it was halted or curtailed by the State. A sense, then, of rupture.

I spoke to Alexander Semyonov, Associate Dean for international students, to ask him for books in English to read about Russian history; he gave me a list of titles.

I remembered only last night that my parents were married on shipboard on the way to Russia as students in 1936. I do not know to where they traveled; Moscow, I believe, but am not sure. Where did they sail from and where did they land?

Seagulls are crying; a whine and then a loud high sigh.

Smoking is not prohibited.

TUESDAY

Went to the Hermitage, a massive, pale green presence, set in an open space; generous, grand. Lines were forming, but the museum was not yet open. Mostly tourists from Japan and Germany and Russia; very few Americans. Many large groups with guides. I went immediately into the shop, having bought a ticket, and stood for a while looking at the various possibilities; mostly too expensive, but I got a lovely scarf for J. When I returned to the hall, there was Noah Chasin, who teaches at Bard, with his pregnant wife Michelle, and so we went through the vast rooms together. It is wildly extravagant in its proportions, with huge chandeliers and scads of gilt. The walls are painted a grassy green. We spent most time with Rembrandt; the *Depo-*

sition an astonishing painting: Jesus heavy and totally human, being lifted down from the cross, his flesh sagging. And the portrait of the old Jew, his hands swollen with arthritis, his face a miracle of intelligent sadness. And the somewhat murky, varnished *Return of the Prodigal Son*, with the passage from Luke: *"his father saw him, and had compassion, and ran, and kissed him."* The cadence of this line struck me.

Many too many paintings to take in, cascades of them, some poorly lit, or lit in such a way that there is only glare, as with the Monets. Many *objets* as well, mosaic floors, huge golden peacocks. At last we got to Matisse, too late to dwell, but first another shop, where Michelle perked up and bought two beautiful amber necklaces; I bought one, maybe for N., maybe for me. *The Conversation* is as I recalled, a study in couple rage: Madame Matisse with the strange black mark on her face, her back arched; himself a column without contrition, with the world window between them, in their dark accusatory silence. What did she say? *"You slept with her, didn't you?"*

The Dance also, and *Music*, with the set of orange figures on a green scumbled ground.

And the beautiful portrait of Madame Matisse, in blues and mauves, in her pretty hat.

I got lost on return, somehow took a wrong turn, and walked long streets until I finally got back to the hotel, sweaty and footsore. I have eaten practically nothing. Tonight there is a reading; I will go to it, and maybe find someone with whom to have dinner.

So far, it is strangely solitary in terms of the others at SLS. Slept for almost two hours.

And missed the first faculty reading, so I could in fact have gone back to Smolny for commencement. We were meant to meet in the lobby at six, but I was barely awake. *La*. This missing of events seems to be becoming ingrained in my subconscious, and I don't quite know what to do about it. It seems to be a decision I have not actively made.

I bought a few things in the small food shop downstairs, but the women there are impatient with my lack of Russian language, and do not take kindly to any hesitation. I feel embarrassed and a little annoyed, wishing for some of that American open disposition, the urban New Yorker's inclination to help. All the encounters I have had with Russians have been curt and abrupt, to say the least. One has a sense of deeply held suspicions, a basic inwardness or a long trajectory of public spaces not used for social contact; the opposite in this respect from, say, Paris. The infestation of cell phones has not happened yet.

Up this morning at 5:30; I slept hours and hours. Managed to make an excellent cup of coffee, with milk!

Heaven.

Very little to eat.

Began to read the poems of my students. Depressing really. The Idea of the Poem overshadows the poem. Some of them have a need to say something, have something to convey, but their linguistic aptitude— their sense of language as medium, as material—is underdeveloped.

Cadence, sound structure. Information dominates over any other idea of sense-making.

Why didn't I bring my little dictionary?

Suddenly thinking of Merrill's *The Changing Light at Sandover*, the title more than the poem, looking out at the domed church, its cross sideways as the sun that never set rises. Wishing I had a really good camera, wanting to be able to capture the details of the pictorial.

Back now from class and lunch, feeling more tired than any time since I arrived. Very hot. Skipped the Dostoevsky tour but will catch it next week, and now am going to take a nap, maybe get up in time to go to the

Church of the Spilled Blood, then to dinner with Mat-
thew Zapruder and his lady.

Slept two hours or so, and still feel groggy and slightly
off—as if I were maybe getting sick also, as others have
been. So, in fact, *nothing to say.*

THURSDAY

Slept until 11—now my internal clock is totally confused.

Drank many glasses of white wine last night and had
my first good meal of grilled salmon.

It is raining: *idyot dozhd.* Fragment recalled from
college Russian.

Learned a little more last night from melancholy
Mikhail about Saint Petersburg; mainly, that the beau-
tiful young women in their tight clothes and high heels
one sees strutting are, according to him, hoping to be
seen by a rich Westerner and taken to America to live
happily ever after. They are not prostitutes, but women
with a fantasy; they are dressed in a cross between Mi-
ami, Las Vegas, L.A. You feel the influence of, say, John
Galliano, or Versace; especially Versace.

The men are often drunk; he said, for the women, a man
who is not a drunk is like a prince. Also, I have learned
there is a high prevalence of AIDS here, due to dirty

needles. I have not seen anyone reading a newspaper. The salaries are extremely low; the middle class is small but evidently growing; in Moscow, however, I'm told there are sixty-two billionaires and counting, part of the oligarchy that formed, after Perestroika, when powerful persons bought up private industry; much of its resources—oil, clearly. The rest got the leftovers.

A lecture now, at last. But no breakfast.

FRIDAY

In fact two lectures, one, by Matvei Yankelevich, on the early avant-garde theatre here, and one, later, by Komar of Komar and Melamid. Much intellectual enlightenment, to be annotated later, as now I have to shake off a difficult, confusing sleep that has left me feeling difficult and confused. And take a close look at some student poems for today's class. In the day yesterday, the day that is also night, that enters into night like a thief in the night of the night, long walks through this phantom city of someone's—well, Peter's—dream, in which its inhabitants appear to be invaders from another altogether different condition, to not fit in, but to move through its majestic colored façades like extras in a Fellini film not directed by Fellini. If one could say that New Yorkers somehow become New York, or that Parisians more or less define Paris, the inhabitants of Petersburg cause or perform an almost visceral rift with their city. As it faces out, they face inward. As it is all elegance and lingering starless luminosity, pastel, classical, they are closed and quick, suspicious and drunken, driving at terrifying speeds in toxic cars apparently in a great desire toward destruction of someone or something. There was a dog that came along, a cur if ever there was a cur, mangy and miserable, skulking through the grass. There was a woman in black, rumbling through garbage, once beautiful, now vacant and lost. There was a bride, with entourage, in high spiked heels and a hooped gown, her groom on a cellphone as they posed for their picture. The women in the wedding party gaudily dressed, highly made-up, with jewels and satins and exposed flesh. All this at the foot of the statue of Peter on his horse with its trailing snake on a vast granite mound. City of dreams and incipient violence, as if it could at any minute return to the swamp on which it was built.

As with the drivers, there is no street etiquette; no one steps out of your way, no one bothers to excuse himself when bumping into you. Also, there is no smiling at strangers but a blank impassive stare greets each passing interchange; this stare does not seem about to change toward a smile; more likely toward overt hostility. Even the vast open spaces seem without the possibility of a *flaneur's* delight in anonymity, a pleasure always heightened by the possibility of a chance encounter, a serendipitous, lucky shift in the relation to destiny which, to my mind at least, is the essence of the urban. So there seems in the body language a kind of fate, an acceptance of fate, as if everyone were being hurled along on its rapid current. Mobility is not tempered by digression or a change of mind, and so to be lost is to be caught without purpose, at risk. (I need to read Benjamin's *Moscow Diaries*.) Nothing is put into bags: no plastic, no paper: not yet the huge detritus of commerce, but very soon to come. At the market, you can buy a plastic bag from an old woman for a few rubles.

So it goes.

Now it is 11:20 pm; the light in the sky is as if a perfect twilight, the sky pale blue, the air cool; perhaps it is eight or nine in high summer on the East Coast. There is no shifting down, no evening song from the birds; no birds. In the distance, a constant mechanical sound, of a fan, perhaps, and the dim hum of city life. A reading tonight (George Saunders) in another strange venue, with huge bouquets of false flowers on a curtained small stage; the walls green. The Museum of the Theatre. There are many museums, but the life of culture and the life of the city feel at odds; I have yet to recognize on any street at any time the face of enquiry or curiosity. There are no neighborhoods of like-mindedness, since real estate is evidently still dictated by some rules of occupancy not connected to, or dictated by, choice.

I am still amazed by the fact that people in the street crash into you without even the slightest regard, as if you were an inanimate object in the way. The sidewalks on the smaller streets are very narrow, and so this kind of bumbling is frequent. People walk faster here than in New York, as if there were a mass mandate to catch up with some fictive present as it careens into the future; or, perhaps, a desire to race from the past? Same difference.

Genya and I went on a walk, and to the "mall," an upheaval of chaotic merchandise housed in a squalid imitation of glitz; whatever "belongs to Russia" is being quickly erased by a rush to Euro-American stuff. We went up to a small store where she had earlier found some indigenous hand-embroidered linens, only to find a few tea-towels from Belarus; everything else now just the pervasive mass-market junk one could find in any store anywhere.

But then we went to the huge indoor market, where one had a sense of some local agriculture—mounds of fresh cheeses, white and slightly sour, and caviar, and many high tables of foods, but nothing that made you think: this is it, except, perhaps, the plastic vats of honeys, each with a different flavor, offered to taste on small bits of wax paper. I bought a small tub of mountain honey, my favorite, with its rich taste of thyme, lavender, and darkness. This taste throws me back to summer visits to Cadaqués, climbing a mountain with Jackie Monnier, Teeny Duchamp's daughter, to find the farm with mountain honey. Taste as a door to memory. Proust.

Drank excellent pepper vodka; ate a caviar blin, with
Matthew, Anna, Matvei, Genya at a Russian family
restaurant, with the Bear and Masha at the door. I
asked Matvei if the Bear in the story eats Masha.
"Does the bear eat Masha?" Matvei repeated. "I cannot
remember." A gypsy dancer in a ravishing sequined
dress sang but could not be heard, accompanied by two
musicians, also inaudible above the din. A huge man in
green pants. The women, as usual, in tight, revealing
garb, like exotic birds strutting. Masha is Maria is Mary.

It is almost midnight, almost but never.

SATURDAY

Awakened by banging on the door: "Open the door!"
The tall thin blond making rapid motions back and
forth with her hand; she wants the iron, and she wants
it now! Borrowed yesterday, I did not get the chance to
use it, and somehow knew there would be a term to the
lease.

What is the etymology of *modern*?

In a dream, LB, paternal figure who invariably causes
me to want to please him, like a little girl, is indifferent
to me; his new baby girl is being looked after by various
faculty women and he seems also to be indifferent to
her. I wonder now, here in Russia, if this is how I felt
my father's response to me, his second daughter?

31

Women writers haunted by their dead fathers.

And despite my wounded vanity of age, I can see that
without the additional impediment of sexual attraction,
one might be able to register more fully as a person,
as a woman who thinks. I know this already but here
I begin to perceive a certain authority granted, as if,
in order to have it, you have to strip yourself of your
erotic bearings and become, in a sense, beyond gender.
This makes me sad.

Saunders made some nice remarks about writing. He
warned about getting old as a form of prudery, or a
conviction about bestness, about value. He also spoke
about the US as having, after 9/11, retreated to the
shores instead of having the courage to say, "We will
from henceforth try to prevent all suffering everywhere."

Well, this is a form of idealism that belongs to youth,
to revolutionary thinking, to change, a commitment to
change: a commitment to progress as a human rather
than a technological endeavor. The empty vacuous face
of technology intervenes, masks the far more difficult
task of self-consciousness, that is, human conscious-
ness, consciousness of being human, a commitment to
being human. Emerson's "silent melancholy" might ap-
ply here; Thoreau's "quiet desperation." In Russia, it is
everywhere, a kind of frenzy of blindness. No one looks
at anyone in the eye, as if to do so would cause some
kind of fatal eruption. The meaning of consent, or lack
of it, is based on a sense that those in power care about

what the public thinks; in the US, we are in a state in which such listening is void as if, indeed, our leaders were deaf.

If they are deaf, then we need a new kind of sign language.

So we could invoke here Komar's marvelous SOTS ART works, which take up the signs, literally, of propaganda, both as American commercialism and Russian, Soviet, ideology; or even, Saunders' violent critique of advertisement. In both cases, the idea is that these forms of passive consent need to be turned into active contestation, or at least, an awareness that they obscure the activity of assent; they assume it, like positive markers that leave no room for contradiction. One thinks now that all the references to pop culture in recent American art feel hollow and vacuous, since they evoke these signs but do so little to contest or alter them, as if they were just a more convenient discourse from which to draw. (So Warhol, as Komar suggests, remains the great innovator, after Duchamp.)

Does the Bear eat Masha? I have forgotten.

Stanley Cavell, "Milton speaks of the effect of tyranny sitting 'heavy on the commonwealth' as palpable as 'household unhappiness,' and he draws the consequences of this heaviness as dispiritedness and disorder in 'the life of grown men' and the neglect of their children, or generally, on the model of an unhappy marriage, a general absence of conversation. As if society at large had become tacit." *(Cities of Words)*

I am interested in the fact that everyone who speaks here of George Saunders comments on his niceness, and wants to make a direct correlative between this and his dark vision, as if he would have to be a melancholy misanthrope in order to write what he writes. This is a typical confusion, isn't it? Surely his work is embedded in cultural perception rather than personal evocation—"self-expression"—in which the imagination, ah, the imagination, is asked to enter into the act of making.

Midnight on its way again. The swallows are torquing through the courtyard zapping mosquitoes and making that strange high-pitched thin whistle. Another sound unrealizable in words. Went for a massage today with Genya; a big Russian, with incredibly strong hands that at times seemed not like hands at all, worked my back and neck and arms and scalp. It was an amazing physical encounter, without any exchange of words. I think I feel better. Then a brief respite, then the ballet, *Romeo and Juliet*, with an assorted audience, and an announcement in four languages about cell phones and photographs. Persons in their fineries. Some Americans.

The dancing was ok, nothing really amazing, except for one man who seemed to be more horse than man; I disliked both Romeo and Juliet as dancers. The sets were fine, except it all seemed slightly caged and reactionary, like a quotation from Russian ballet.

I left after the second act, feeling not very involved except for some moments, and tired, and wanting something to eat, and so walked through the crowded streets back to the Pub across the street, where some of the SLS folks were to be found, watching soccer, including Tony from Ghana, a small, vivid, intelligent man, full of mischief and almost impossibly gregarious, with his team playing and winning against the Czechs. I had three glasses of white wine and two small delicious salads, which set me back 1000 rubles. Met some more students. Smoked. Talked. You could become mad here, desolate and dissolute, without any work, and then, when winter comes, you would find yourself in hell.

SUNDAY A.M.

Sebald *(Campo Santo)* writes that Nietzsche, thinking about mnemonic techniques in the *Genealogy of Morals*, "thought there was nothing more sinister in the prehistory of mankind than the combination of pain and recollection to construct a memory. But what is taken from the living substance of the individual in the long process of his training to become an articulate, moral human being adheres to the linguistic machine until in the end the parts become interchangeable in function."

(One could make an interesting compendium of writing about the machine, ending perhaps with Deleuze.)

mode modality model

Sebald continues (he is writing about Handke's play *Kaspar*), "speech is an apparatus run out of control and beginning to lead a sinister life of its own. Model sentences such as those suggested to Kaspar are reflexes of the cruel treatment to which his sensory apparatus is submitted by its linguistic shaping."

These distortions interest me. Torture, for example, could arrest or alter linguistic sense into violent shapes. A maudlin tangle of words that so ruptures the machine of language that when it begins again to make sense one feels a new gladness or relief. If we have now a globalizing machine that moves with such rapid stealth, arriving in Saint Petersburg with its Logos (a kind of hidden history, or prehistory), then there must be a way to create a poetics that captures this combination of access and obscurity. Take, for example, the store Strawberry, which sells cheap sports clothes for teenagers. I remember, when I first saw the name and the big strawberry logo, I thought it was a ridiculous brand name. But now, walking along the street, I see in the window an enormous strawberry in a clothing store, and realize that, of course, this would be a brand that would move quickly across cultures, carrying notions of bright! Fresh!

I could not find my lighter last night. Tony went to get me a light, but took a cigarette to the bar, lit it, and then began to smoke it when he returned to the table. Later, he went to make a phone call—he was gone for a long time—and when he came back, he handed me a red cricket lighter, saying that I could keep it. But my lighter is in fact a red cricket lighter, and I have awakened thinking that he is a kind of Trickster. As we were talking, he made some remark about "his connection," and then protested, "I am clean, I am clean," but I think there is some possibility he is not, and that part of his gregariousness is augmented. These are not positive thoughts, and I feel ashamed of them. Long phone calls in bars perhaps triggered a memory of deception. And he has about him the air of subversion.

And I now have two red cricket lighters. *Double your pleasure, double your fun.*

I feel so glad to be away from the immediacy of our debacle.

Handke: *I am the one I am.*

Homer (Odysseus): *I am Nobody.*

Dickinson: *I am nobody. Who are you?*

Stein: *I am I because my little dog knows me.*

Stevens: *I am as I am*—how does that go?—*As I am I am?*

The empty shifter.

Identical.

Does it make any sense to read a book one can read
anywhere if one is somewhere one may never be again?

If the "one" in the Handke quote means "only," then it
could be "I am the only I am."

Went to the Russian Museum, not very successfully,
today; that is, I feel I did not see what was there to be
seen and so I will have to return, at least for the icons.
Only a few Kandinsky, unless I missed them, and only
a few Malevich. Many French-inspired nineteenth-
century Impressionisms, and hundreds of pre-Soviet
history paintings and portraits, some of the former on
a giant scale, and quite powerful. Also strange encoun-
ters between Christ and Russia, along with portraits of
Lenin and depictions of the Revolution.

But then there was a reading, or a manifestation, at
Stray Dog, the café where Mayakovsky et al. gathered,
shut down, and reopened a decade ago, of the last Rus-
sian avant-garde, the OBERIU group—I know nothing
of these persons or their work, so this was a kind of
revelation or awakening. Perhaps in particular Daniil
Kharms (d.1942), but most particularly the poem by

Alexander Vvedensky that contains the phrase "the pebble of death" and "I regret that I am not a rug or a hydrangea." There are other regrets and some refrains of regrets, and an incantatory ode-like motion that is not reminiscent of anything I know. And a play, a conversation about the absence of poetry, which of course turns into the presence of poetry at its most sublimely absurd: reckless and sorrowful, comic and wistful, with undercurrents of some incalculable set of feelings and knowledge to which I at present have no access. An "intellectual circus."

There are no birds here.
Are there birds here?

MONDAY A.M.

Slept poorly. And, for the first time I actually know what *white nights* refer to: the sky turns a pale white, like a pearl under mist.

It is another kind of mystery, but I do miss the moon and stars; do they appear in Russian iconography; certainly they appear in poems? In winter, is there a nearly constant radiant firmament?

I am recalling the Easter egg my father brought back, with its inscription on the inside, now barely visible. Does the egg replace the moon?

There are no stars here.
Are there stars here?

I love finding history through conversation, its peculiar
fragmentation and shaped perspective, augmented by
observation. I love walking along and having someone
(Matvei) tell me that the building on Nevsky Prospect,
ornate with a glassed-in cupola and smaller globe on
top, and floating projecting angels, was where these po-
ets gathered, where there had been an immense book-
store and, before that, was the Singer Sewing Machine
building! Now it stands empty, ready for Disney.

Does the Bear eat Masha? I have forgotten.

It is still Sunday in New York.

MONDAY P.M.

OK class. Still, a strange muteness follows from it, no
après, but a sudden dispersal, so I do not quite know
how to measure its effects, its usefulness.

Just returned from a talk about Russian Symbolism,
and the novel *Petersburg* by Andrei Bely, written first
in 1916. A great rambling talk in which I gleaned a few
cornerstones. Geometry, mysticism, idea and mind:
not based on empiricism but on something both more
absolute and yet more hidden, as in Gnosticism, be-
yond appearances. The character "Petersburg" not held

by foundations and histories, but as in a stage set, a theater.

An opera singer is practicing; her voice echoing into the courtyard.

TUESDAY A.M.

I seem to have lost the night.

Wondering about how habits break, and then, slowly, come back again. Something about the elasticity of the psyche. Its capacity to expand, shift, renew. I will not have made friends here because I do not join in the various group events. So yesterday. And here, in this journal, I see myself coming back into focus as the subject; Saint Petersburg begins already to withdraw. It is a demanding, unforgiving city.

So one can go without eating if one has a dread of sitting in public alone.

Honey for dinner.

Cigarettes and coffee for breakfast. The milk is sour.

The heat now is heavier, more humid.

I need to go back to a museum.

I miss my garden, I miss my cat.

Geometry. Absolute Truth because unchanging, ahistorical. The circle and the square and the line never change, have neither face nor incident. Pure abstraction then represents the Mind of God who does not have any specific attributes either, but is an idealism. The subject-object divide is perhaps disintegrated in this more vertical (medieval?) reading, and so syntax and linear argument, plot, are forsaken for fragments of mobility, mobile fragments. The real cannot be rendered as language; language is a separate, homogenous, reality.

How many kinds of fragments are there, Dear Professor?

I take this—what is this? Saint Petersburg as a trope for Geometry—to be something about the way the rational cannot be imposed from without, if the within has a disposition toward spirituality. If Saint Petersburg represents the Enlightenment in the hands of the State, then what happens to those habits of unreason, of faith and belief? These are questions that also haunt America; maybe they haunt the entire West.

FRIDAY 22 JUNE

Now it, or this, is almost memory, the great subtractor. Experience minus presence equals memory.

Yesterday: the class, more Untranslatable Russia, the frenzy of amber buying, some food at the "Office," the mock English pub across the street, a somewhat pro-tracted presentation/reading by Ugly Duckling Presse, in Russian and English (three living Russian poets), some food, and a midnight boat ride along the canal to the river, to celebrate the solstice.

Hallucinatory, the façades along the banks more ir-real than ever, the sky pale and then, around 2:30 am, changing into a deep impossible blue.

Petersburg is fabulous, as in *fable,* a kind of closed circuit of powerful significations wrapped around a setting that appears without historical purchase or, rather, to have only historical purchase that has re-sisted alteration. The Russian obsession, if I can call it that, with the materiality/spirituality duality; with the object as such, the thing itself. Icons.

The desire to strip things of the desire for them, to somehow prevent their contamination by capital, ex-change: *all that is solid melts into air.*

You can see why film would have become important, with its sheen of light and shadow flickering in the artificial dark. It must now be a cliché to say that Pe-tersburg is like a film set. But the boat ride only inten-sified this sense, with all the extras, the citizens, lined up along the banks. There were, in fact, many boats moving slowly as if in a herd. The buildings show no signs of wear, that is one way in which this paltry comparison is true, their magnificent classical frontages pristine and illumined; green and gold and paprika and white, these make the human to be mere, flimsy and insubstantial, and yet they, these buildings, are also somehow weightless as if suspended or propped up. One could imagine walking through one of the many arches to find oneself in a field or a forest.

Does the Bear eat Masha? I have forgotten.

Today I am going back to the Russian Museum to see the icons. Tonight I am reading.

Almost no political talk while here, as if we all want to forget what is happening in the world; or perhaps, there is nothing to say.

And the World Cup is a constant.

SUNDAY 25 JUNE NYC

Home again home again jiggidy jog.

The last two days escape narration, become a blur. A visit to the icons to see the distillation of time. A visit to the Akhmatova museum to see another rendition of the distillation of time; the former, within the iconography of faith, the miracles of saints, George and Peter, Gabriel and the Mother of God, no depictions of the

Crucifix as far as I recall but the presence everywhere of deep brilliant crimson as of fresh blood. Akhmatova's house a memorial to a life, with postcards and scraps of paper; with her kitchen and her desk, the objects now haunted by having been part of living presences. This is the blue jug she used to pour water. This is the chair where she sat. The ragged ephemera of a life. I think of Dickinson in Amherst. What a contrast.

Our (Matthew Zapruder, Eugene and my) reading was in the same room at the American Corner, this time almost impossibly hot. I said, "I regret I am not a fan or an air-conditioner." *I regret I am not a rug or a hydrangea.* I read third and last into the sweltering crowd, the reading curtailed by the heat.

During the final class I broke down weeping after an exchange with a student. I was speaking about the dangers of poetry being absorbed into the academy; how the academic is anathema to the poetic because the ground of knowledge for poetry is necessarily different from that of the academic, the scholar. Scholars must believe that subjects have epistemological orders; there is depth of field, there is a built-in limit to the extent of facts, since most scholars move from the past into the present and back again, the present being only that which conducts the inquiry; it changes with its theoretical frame, its interpretive tools, its methodology. For poets, the present is the subject itself, it is the ordering frame, the frame of relation, and knowledge comes to the place of the poem only in terms of that present and its demands. Any fact or situation or text is possibly conjunct to the poem, any history, building; any incident. Poets are not scholars because there cannot be a discrete subject, a specific site of knowing. Thus poets are scanners allowing whatever to surface up from the deep primordial conditions of the living word. Icons, Anna Akhmatova, bird. We must always reconstrue and reconstruct the materials of timespace in order to give life to the present. This is what Celan is talking about when he says the poem asserts the *still here.*

The student challenged me, she said I was being as categorical as what I was attacking, and I began to weep. She seemed to suggest that my antagonism was personal, a result of having been mistreated at the hands of the academy. This is not true, except for the fact that the academy disdains to write any serious criticism of my work, a fact I take to be at least in part because of my investment in the present and the ways in which my knowledge is absorbed into the materials of the poem rather than riding on its surface like a trophy or proof. We do not need to have Benjamin's Angel of History staring us in the face. I had said something quite nasty about academics wanting the good life—security and nice houses and all that, but I did not say that my problem is not with those desires, which I share, but with the sense that they are entitled to these things, that they come with the territory, an assumption about bourgeois privilege which has begun to infiltrate poetic judgment. This part of my argument is unclear.

On my last night, dinner at a Georgian restaurant with Anna, Matvei and Genya, my dear companions. And a final drink at the Pub, at which Eugene joined us. He asked me about how I knew Michael Palmer, and I told the story of inviting Michael to read for my class at City College, and of his arriving at the door at Duane Street, and my opening the door to this handsome man in jeans and a leather jacket, and his saying "Hi."

Ann Lauterbach, poet and essayist, is the author of nine books of poetry, a collection of essays, and numerous works on and with visual artists. She is co-Chair of Writing in the Milton Avery Graduate School of the Arts and Schwab Professor of Languages and Literature at Bard College. She lives in Germantown, New York.